Lo

SIR WALTER SCO

A Phoenix Paperback

This abridged edition published in 1996 by Phoenix
a division of Orion Books Ltd
Orion House, 5 Upper St Martin's Lane, London WC2H 9EA

Cover illustration: 'The Betrothal of Robert Burns and Highland Mary' by
James Archer, Forbes Magazine Collection (Bridgeman Art
Library, London)

ISBN 1 85799 673 9

Typeset by Deltatype Ltd, Ellesmere Port, Cheshire
Printed in Great Britain by
Clays Ltd, St Ives plc.

CONTENTS

from 'MARMION'

Lochinvar

O, young Lochinvar is come out of the west,
Through all the wide Border his steed was the best;
And save his good broadsword he weapons had none,
He rode all unarm'd, and he rode all alone.
So faithful in love, and so dauntless in war,
There never was knight like the young Lochinvar.

He staid not for brake, and he stopp'd not for stone,
He swam the Eske river where ford there was none;
But ere he alighted at Netherby gate,
The bride had consented, the gallant came late:
For a laggard in love, and a dastard in war,
Was to wed the fair Ellen of brave Lochinvar.

So boldly he enter'd the Netherby Hall,
Among bride's-men, and kinsmen, and brothers, and all:
Then spoke the bride's father, his hand on his sword,
(For the poor craven bridegroom said never a word,)

'O come ye in peace here, or come ye in war,
Or to dance at our bridal, young Lord Lochinvar?'

'I long woo'd your daughter, my suit you denied; –
Love swells like the Solway, but ebbs like its tide –
And now am I come, with this lost love of mine,
To lead but one measure, drink one cup of wine.
There are maidens in Scotland more lovely by far,
That would gladly be bride to the young Lochinvar.'

The bride kiss'd the goblet: the knight took it up,
He quaff'd off the wine, and he threw down the cup.
She look'd down to blush, and she look'd up to sigh,
With a smile on her lips, and a tear in her eye.
He took her soft hand, ere her mother could bar, –
'Now tread we a measure!' said young Lochinvar.

So stately his form, and so lovely her face,
That never a hall such a galliard did grace;
While her mother did fret, and her father did fume,
And the bridegroom stood dangling his bonnet and plume;
And the bride-maidens whisper'd, ''Twere better by far,
To have match'd our fair cousin with young Lochinvar.'

One touch to her hand, and one word in her ear,
When they reach'd the hall door, and the charger stood
        near;
So light to the croupe the fair lady he swung,

So light to the saddle before her he sprung!
'She is won! we are gone, over bank, bush, and scaur;
They'll have fleet steeds that follow,' quoth young
  Lochinvar.

There was mounting 'mong Græmes of the Netherby clan;
Forsters, Fenwicks, and Musgraves, they rode and they ran:
There was racing and chasing on Cannobie Lee,
But the lost bride of Netherby ne'er did they see.
So daring in love, and so dauntless in war,
Have ye e'er heard of gallant like young Lochinvar? –

from 'THE LAY OF THE LAST MINSTREL'

The Minstrel

The way was long, the wind was cold,
The Minstrel was infirm and old;
His wither'd cheek, and tresses gray,
Seem'd to have known a better day;
The harp, his sole remaining joy,
Was carried by an orphan boy.
The last of all the Bards was he,
Who sung of Border chivalry;
For, welladay! their date was fled,
His tuneful brethren all were dead;
And he, neglected and oppress'd,
Wish'd to be with them, and at rest.
No more on prancing palfrey borne,
He caroll'd, light as lark at morn;
No longer courted and caress'd,
High placed in hall, a welcome guest,
He pour'd to lord and lady gay
The unpremeditated lay:

Old times were changed, old manners gone;
A stranger fill'd the Stuarts' throne;
The bigots of the iron time
Had call'd his harmless art a crime.
A wandering Harper, scorn'd and poor,
He begg'd his bread from door to door,
And tuned, to please a peasant's ear,
The harp a king had loved to hear.

He pass'd where Newark's stately tower
Looks out from Yarrow's birchen bower:
The Minstrel gazed with wishful eye –
No humbler resting-place was nigh;
With hesitating step at last
The embattled portal arch he pass'd,
Whose ponderous grate and massy bar
Had oft roll'd back the tide of war,
But never closed the iron door
Against the desolate and poor.
The Duchess mark'd his weary pace,
His timid mien, and reverend face,
And bade her page the menials tell
That they should tend the old man well:
For she had known adversity,
Though born in such a high degree;
In pride of power, in beauty's bloom,
Had wept o'er Monmouth's bloody tomb!

When kindness had his wants supplied,
And the old man was gratified,
Began to rise his minstrel pride:
And he began to talk anon
Of good Earl Francis, dead and gone,
And of Earl Walter, rest him, God!
A braver ne'er to battle rode;
And how full many a tale he knew
Of the old warriors of Buccleuch:
And, would the noble Duchess deign
To listen to an old man's strain,
Though stiff his hand, his voice though weak,
He thought even yet, the sooth to speak,
That, if she loved the harp to hear,
He could make music to her ear.

The humble boon was soon obtain'd;
The aged Minstrel audience gain'd.
But, when he reach'd the room of state,
Where she with all her ladies sate,
Perchance he wish'd his boon denied:
For, when to tune his harp he tried,
His trembling hand had lost the ease,
Which marks security to please;
And scenes long past, of joy and pain,
Came wildering o'er his aged brain –
He tried to tune his harp in vain!
The pitying Duchess prais'd its chime,

And gave him heart, and gave him time,
Till every string's according glee
Was blended into harmony.
And then, he said, he would full fain
He could recall an ancient strain
He never thought to sing again.
It was not framed for village churls,
But for high dames and mighty earls;
He had play'd it to King Charles the Good,
When he kept court in Holyrood;
And much he wish'd, yet fear'd, to try
The long-forgotten melody.
Amid the strings his fingers stray'd,
And an uncertain warbling made,
And oft he shook his hoary head.
But when he caught the measure wild,
The old man rais'd his face, and smil'd;
And lighten'd up his faded eye
With all a poet's ecstasy.
In varying cadence, soft or strong,
He swept the sounding chords along:
The present scene, the future lot,
His toils, his wants, were all forgot;
Cold diffidence, and age's frost,
In the full tide of song were lost;
Each blank, in faithless memory void,
The poet's glowing thought supplied;
And, while his harp responsive rung,
'Twas thus the Latest Minstrel sung.

Melrose Abbey

If thou would'st view fair Melrose aright,
Go visit it by the pale moonlight;
For the gay beams of lightsome day
Gild, but to flout, the ruins grey.
When the broken arches are black in night,
And each shafted oriel glimmers white;
When the cold light's uncertain shower
Streams on the ruin'd central tower;
When buttress and buttress, alternately,
Seem fram'd of ebon and ivory;
When silver edges the imagery,
And the scrolls that teach thee to live and die;
When distant Tweed is heard to rave,
And the owlet to hoot o'er the dead man's grave,
Then go – but go alone the while –
Then view St David's ruin'd pile;
And, home returning, soothly swear,
Was never scene so sad and fair!

Love

In peace, Love tunes the shepherd's reed;
In war, he mounts the warrior's steed;
In halls, in gay attire is seen:
In hamlets, dances on the green.
Love rules the court, the camp, the grove,
And men below, and saints above;
For love is heaven, and heaven is love.

Nature's sympathy with the poet

Call it not vain; they do not err,
   Who say, that when the Poet dies,
Mute Nature mourns her worshipper,
   And celebrates his obsequies:
Who say, tall cliff and cavern lone
For the departed Bard make moan;
That mountains weep in crystal rill;
That flowers in tears of balm distil;
Through his lov'd groves that breezes sigh,
And oaks, in deeper groan, reply;
And rivers teach their rushing wave
To murmur dirges round his grave.

Not that, in sooth, o'er mortal urn
Those things inanimate can mourn;

But that the stream, the wood, the gale,
Is vocal with the plaintive wail
Of those, who, else forgotten long,
Liv'd in the poet's faithful song,
And, with the poet's parting breath,
Whose memory feels a second death.
The Maid's pale shade, who wails her lot,
That love, true love, should be forgot,
From rose and hawthorn shakes the tear
Upon the gentle Minstrel's bier:
The phantom Knight, his glory fled,
Mourns o'er the field he heap'd with dead;
Mounts the wild blast that sweeps amain,
And shrieks along the battle-plain.
The Chief, whose antique crownlet long
Still sparkled in the feudal song,
Now, from the mountain's misty throne,
Sees, in the thanedom once his own,
His ashes undistinguish'd lie,
His place, his power, his memory die:
His groans the lonely caverns fill,
His tears of rage impel the rill:
All mourn the Minstrel's harp unstrung,
Their name unknown, their praise unsung.

'True love's the gift which God has given'

True love's the gift which God has given
To man alone beneath the heaven:
   It is not fantasy's hot fire,
      Whose wishes, soon as granted, fly;
   It liveth not in fierce desire,
      With dead desire it doth not die;
It is the secret sympathy,
The silver link, the silken tie,
Which heart to heart, and mind to mind,
In body and in soul can bind.

'Breathes there the man, with soul so dead'

Breathes there the man, with soul so dead,
Who never to himself hath said,
   This is my own, my native land!
Whose heart hath ne'er within him burn'd,
As home his footsteps he hath turn'd,
   From wandering on a foreign strand!
If such there breathe, go, mark him well;
For him no Minstrel raptures swell;
High though his titles, proud his name,
Boundless his wealth as wish can claim;
Despite those titles, power, and pelf,
The wretch, concentred all in self,

Living, shall forfeit fair renown,
And, doubly dying, shall go down
To the vile dust, from whence he sprung,
Unwept, unhonour'd, and unsung.

The Dirge of Lovely Rosabelle

O listen, listen, ladies gay!
   No haughty feat of arms I tell;
Soft is the note, and sad the lay,
   That mourns the lovely Rosabelle.

– 'Moor, moor the barge, ye gallant crew!
   And, gentle ladye, deign to stay!
Rest thee in Castle Ravensheuch,
   Nor tempt the stormy firth today.

'The blackening wave is edg'd with white:
   To inch and rock the sea-mews fly;
The fishers have heard the Water-Sprite,
   Whose screams forebode that wreck is nigh.

'Last night the gifted Seer did view
   A wet shroud swathed round ladye gay;
Then stay thee, Fair, in Ravensheuch:
   Why cross the gloomy firth today?'

"'Tis not because Lord Lindesay's heir
    To-night at Roslin leads the ball,
But that my ladye-mother there
    Sits lonely in her castle-hall.

"'Tis not because the ring they ride,
    And Lindesay at the ring rides well,
But that my sire the wine will chide,
    If 'tis not fill'd by Rosabelle.'

O'er Roslin all that dreary night
    A wondrous blaze was seen to gleam;
'Twas broader than the watch-fire's light,
    And redder than the bright moonbeam.

It glar'd on Roslin's castled rock,
    It ruddied all the copse-wood glen;
'Twas seen from Dryden's groves of oak,
    And seen from cavern'd Hawthornden.

Seem'd all on fire that chapel proud,
    Where Roslin's chiefs uncoffin'd lie,
Each Baron, for a sable shroud,
    Sheath'd in his iron panoply.

Seem'd all on fire within, around,
    Deep sacristy and altar's pale;
Shone every pillar foliage-bound,
    And glimmer'd all the dead men's mail.

Blaz'd battlement and pinnet high,
   Blaz'd every rose-carved buttress fair –
So still they blaze when fate is nigh
   The lordly line of high St Clair.

There are twenty of Roslin's barons bold
   Lie buried within that proud chapelle;
Each one the holy vault doth hold –
   But the sea holds lovely Rosabelle!

And each St Clair was buried there,
   With candle, with book, and with knell;
But the sea-caves rung, and the wild winds sung,
   The dirge of lovely Rosabelle.

'The Minstrel's lowly bower'

Hush'd is the harp: the Minstrel gone.
And did he wander forth alone?
Alone, in indigence and age,
To linger out his pilgrimage?
No: close beneath proud Newark's tower,
Arose the Minstrel's lowly bower;
A simple hut; but there was seen
The little garden hedged with green,
The cheerful hearth, and lattice clean.
There shelter'd wanderers, by the blaze,

Oft heard the tale of other days;
For much he lov'd to ope his door,
And give the aid he begg'd before.
So pass'd the winter's day; but still,
When summer smil'd on sweet Bow hill,
And July's eve, with balmy breath,
Wav'd the blue-bells on Newark heath;
When throstles sung in Hareheadshaw,
And corn was green on Carterhaugh,
And flourish'd broad Blackandro's oak,
The aged Harper's soul awoke!
Then would he sing achievements high,
And circumstance of chivalry,
Till the rapt traveller would stay,
Forgetful of the closing day;
And noble youths, the strain to hear,
Forsook the hunting of the deer;
And Yarrow, as he roll'd along,
Bore burden to the Minstrel's song.

from 'THE LADY OF THE LAKE'

Boat Song – 'Hail to the Chief'

'Hail to the Chief who in triumph advances!
    Honour'd and bless'd be the evergreen Pine!
Long may the tree, in his banner that glances,
    Flourish, the shelter and grace of our line!
        Heaven send it happy dew,
        Earth lend it sap anew,
Gayly to bourgeon, and broadly to grow,
        While every Highland glen
        Sends our shout back agen,
Roderigh Vich Alpine dhu, ho! ieroe!

'Ours is no sapling, chance-sown by the fountain,
    Blooming at Beltane, in winter to fade;
When the whirlwind has stripp'd every leaf on the
      mountain,
    The more shall Clan-Alpine exult in her shade.
        Moor'd in the rifted rock,
        Proof to the tempest's shock,

Firmer he roots him the ruder it blow;
 Menteith and Breadalbane, then,
 Echo his praise agen,
Roderigh Vich Alpine dhu, ho! ieroe!

'Proudly our pibroch has thrill'd in Glen Fruin,
 And Bannochar's groans to our slogan replied;
Glen Luss and Ross-dhu, they are smoking in ruin,
 And the best of Loch Lomond lie dead on her side.
  Widow and Saxon maid
  Long shall lament our raid,
Think of Clan-Alpine with fear and with woe;
  Lennox and Leven-glen
  Shake when they hear agen,
Roderigh Vich Alpine dhu, ho! ieroe!

'Row, vassals, row, for the pride of the Highlands!
 Stretch to your oars, for the evergreen Pine!
O! that the rose-bud that graces yon islands
 Were wreathed in a garland around him to twine!
  O that some seedling gem,
  Worthy such noble stem,
Honour'd and bless'd in their shadow might grow!
  Loud should Clan-Alpine then
  Ring from her deepmost glen,
Roderigh Vich Alpine dhu, ho! ieroe!'

Coronach

'He is gone on the mountain,
  He is lost to the forest,
Like a summer-dried fountain,
  When our need was the sorest.
The font, reappearing,
  From the rain-drops shall borrow,
But to us comes no cheering,
  To Duncan no morrow!

The hand of the reaper
  Takes the ears that are hoary,
But the voice of the weeper
  Wails manhood in glory.
The autumn winds rushing
  Waft the leaves that are searest,
But our flower was in flushing,
  When blighting was nearest.

Fleet foot on the correi,
  Sage counsel in cumber,
Red hand in the foray,
  How sound is thy slumber!
Like the dew on the mountain,
  Like the foam on the river,
Like the bubble on the fountain,
  Thou art gone, and for ever!'

'The Heath this night must be my bed'

'The heath this night must be my bed,
The bracken curtain for my head,
My lullaby the warder's tread,
    Far, far from love and thee, Mary;
To-morrow eve, more stilly laid,
My couch may be my bloody plaid,
My vesper song, thy wail, sweet maid!
    It will not waken me, Mary!

I may not, dare not, fancy now
The grief that clouds thy lovely brow,
I dare not think upon thy vow,
    And all it promised me, Mary.
No fond regrets must Norman know;
When bursts Clan-Alpine on the foe,
His heart must be like bended bow,
    His foot like arrow free, Mary.

A time will come with feeling fraught,
For, if I fall in battle fought,
Thy hapless lover's dying thought
    Shall be a thought on thee, Mary.
And if return'd from conquer'd foes,
How blithely will the evening close,
How sweet the linnet sing repose,
    To my young bride and me, Mary!'

The Ballad of Alice Brand

Merry it is in the good greenwood,
  When the mavis and merle are singing,
When the deer sweeps by, and the hounds are in cry,
  And the hunter's horn is ringing.

'O Alice Brand, my native land
  Is lost for love of you;
And we must hold by wood and wold,
  As outlaws wont to do.

'O Alice, 'twas all for thy locks so bright,
  And 'twas all for thine eyes so blue,
That on the night of our luckless flight
  Thy brother bold I slew.

'Now must I teach to hew the beech
  The hand that held the glaive,
For leaves to spread our lowly bed,
  And stakes to fence our cave.

'And for vest of pall, thy fingers small,
  That wont on harp to stray,
A cloak must shear from the slaughter'd deer,
  To keep the cold away.'

'O Richard! if my brother died,
    'Twas but a fatal chance;
For darkling was the battle tried,
    And fortune sped the lance.

'If pall and vair no more I wear,
    Nor thou the crimson sheen,
As warm, we'll say, is the russet grey,
    As gay the forest-green.

'And, Richard, if our lot be hard,
    And lost thy native land,
Still Alice has her own Richard,
    And he his Alice Brand.'

'Tis merry, 'tis merry, in good greenwood,
    So blithe Lady Alice is singing;
On the beech's pride, and oak's brown side,
    Lord Richard's axe is ringing.

Up spoke the moody Elfin King,
    Who won'd within the hill;
Like wind in the porch of a ruin'd church,
    His voice was ghostly shrill.

'Why sounds yon stroke on beech and oak,
    Our moonlight circle's screen?
Or who comes here to chase the deer,
    Beloved of our Elfin Queen?

Or who may dare on wold to wear
    The fairies' fatal green?

'Up, Urgan, up! to yon mortal hie,
    For thou wert christen'd man;
For cross or sign thou wilt not fly,
    For mutter'd word or ban.

'Lay on him the curse of the wither'd heart,
    The curse of the sleepless eye;
Till he wish and pray that his life would part,
    Not yet find leave to die.'

'Tis merry, 'tis merry, in good greenwood,
    Though the birds have still'd their singing;
The evening blaze doth Alice raise,
    And Richard is fagots bringing.

Up Urgan starts, that hideous dwarf,
    Before Lord Richard stands,
And, as he cross'd and bless'd himself,
'I fear not sign,' quoth the grisly elf,
    'That is made with bloody hands.'

But out then spoke she, Alice Brand,
    That woman, void of fear, –
'And if there's blood upon his hand,
    'Tis but the blood of deer.'

'Now loud thou liest, thou bold of mood!
    It cleaves unto his hand,
The stain of thine own kindly blood,
    The blood of Ethert Brand.'

Then forward stepp'd she, Alice Brand,
    And made the holy sign, –
'And if there's blood on Richard's hand,
    A spotless hand is mine.

'And I conjure thee, Demon elf,
    By Him whom Demons fear,
To show us whence thou art thyself,
    And what thine errand here?'

''Tis merry, 'tis merry, in Fairy-land,
    When fairy birds are singing,
When the court doth ride by their monarch's side,
    With bit and bridle ringing:

'And gaily shines the Fairy-land –
    But all is glistening show,
Like the idle gleam that December's beam
    Can dart on ice and snow.

'And fading, like that varied gleam,
    Is our inconstant shape,
Who now like knight and lady seem,
    And now like dwarf and ape.

'It was between the night and day,
    When the Fairy King has power,
That I sunk down in a sinful fray,
And, 'twixt life and death, was snatch'd away
    To the joyless Elfin bower.

'But wist I of a woman bold,
    Who thrice my brow durst sign,
I might regain my mortal mold,
    As fair a form as thine.'

She cross'd him once, she cross'd him twice,
    That lady was so brave;
The fouler grew his goblin hue,
    The darker grew the cave.

She cross'd him thrice, that lady bold;
    He rose beneath her hand
The fairest knight on Scottish mold,
    Her brother, Ethert Brand!

Merry it is in good greenwood,
    When the mavis and merle are singing,
But merrier were they in Dunfermline grey,
    When all the bells were ringing.

'Harp of the North, farewell'

Harp of the North, farewell! The hills grow dark,
  On purple peaks a deeper shade descending;
In twilight copse the glow-worm lights her spark,
  The deer, half-seen, are to the covert wending.
Resume thy wizard elm! the fountain lending,
  And the wild breeze, thy wilder minstrelsy;
Thy numbers sweet with nature's vespers blending,
  With distant echo from the fold and lea,
And herd-boy's evening pipe, and hum of housing bee.

Yet once again farewell, thou Mistrel harp!
  Yet once again forgive my feeble sway,
And little reck I of the censure sharp
  May idly cavil at an idle lay.
Much have I owed thy strains on life's long way,
  Through secret woes the world has never known,
When on the weary night dawn'd wearier day,
  And bitterer was the grief devour'd alone.
That I o'erlive such woes, Enchantress! is thine own.

Hark! as my lingering footsteps slow retire,
  Some Spirit of the Air has waked thy string!
'Tis now a seraph bold, with touch of fire,
  'Tis now the brush of Fairy's frolic wing.
Receding now, the dying numbers ring

Fainter and fainter down the rugged dell,
And now the mountain breezes scarcely bring
    A wandering witch-note of the distant spell –
And now, 'tis silent all! – Enchantress, fare thee well!

from 'ROKEBY'

'*O, Brignal banks are wild and fair*'

O, Brignal banks are wild and fair,
And Greta woods are green,
And you may gather garlands there
Would grace a summer queen.

MISCELLANEOUS POEMS

The Eve of Saint John

The Baron of Smaylho'me rose with day,
   He spurr'd his courser on,
Without stop or stay, down the rocky way,
   That leads to Brotherstone.

He went not with the bold Buccleuch,
   His banner broad to rear;
He went not 'gainst the English yew
   To lift the Scottish spear.

Yet his plate-jack was braced, and his helmet was laced,
   And his vaunt-brace of proof he wore;
At his saddle-gerthe was a good steel sperthe,
   Full ten pound weight and more.

The Baron return'd in three days space,
   And his looks were sad and sour;
And weary was his courser's pace,
   As he reach'd his rocky tower.

He came not from where Ancram Moor
    Ran red with English blood;
Where the Douglas true and the bold Buccleuch
    'Gainst keen Lord Evers stood.

Yet was his helmet hack'd and hew'd,
    His acton pierced and tore,
His axe and his dagger with blood imbrued, –
    But it was not English gore.

He lighted at the Chapellage,
    He held him close and still;
And he whistled thrice for his little foot-page,
    His name was English Will.

'Come thou hither, my little foot-page,
    Come hither to my knee;
Though thou art young, and tender of age,
    I think thou art true to me.

'Come, tell me all that thou hast seen,
    And look thou tell me true!
Since I from Saylho'me tower have been,
    What did thy lady do?'

'My lady each night sought the lonely light
    That burns on the wild Watchfold;
For, from height to height, the beacons bright
    Of the English foemen told.

'The bittern clamour'd from the moss,
  The wind blew loud and shrill;
Yet the craggy pathway she did cross
  To the eiry Beacon Hill.

'I watch'd her steps, and silent came
  Where she sat her on a stone;
No watchman stood by the dreary flame,
  It burnèd all alone.

'The second night I kept her in sight
  Till to the fire she came,
And, by Mary's might! an armed Knight
  Stood by the lonely flame.

'And many a word that warlike lord
  Did speak to my lady there;
But the rain fell fast, and loud blew the blast,
  And I heard not what they were.

'The third night there the sky was fair,
  And the mountain-blast wasstill
As again I watch'd the secret pair
  On the lonesome Beacon Hill.

'And I heard her name the midnight hour,
  And name this holy eve,
And say "Come this night to thy lady's bower;
  Ask no bold Baron's l'

' "He lifts his spear with the bold Buccleuch;
   His lady is all alone;
The door she'll undo to her knight so true
   On the eve of good Saint John."

' "I cannot come, I must not come,
   I dare not come to thee;
On the eve of Saint John I must wander alone,
   In thy bower I may not be."

' "Now out on thee, fainthearted knight!
   Thou shouldst not say me nay;
For the eve is sweet, and when lovers meet
   Is worth the whole summer's day.

' "And I'll chain the blood-hound, and the warder shall not
      sound,
   And rushes shall be strew'd on the stair;
So, by the black rood-stone, and by holy Saint John,
   I conjure thee, my love, to be there!"

' "Though the blood-hound be mute, and the rush beneath
      my foot,
   And the warder his bugle should not blow,
Yet there sleepeth a priest in the chamber to the east,
   And my footstep he would know.

' "O fear not the priest, who sleepeth to the east,
   For to Dryburgh the way he has ta'en;

And there to say mass, till three days do pass,
    For the soul of a knight that is slayne."

'He turn'd him around, and grimly he frown'd,
    Then he laugh'd right scornfully –
"He who says the mass-rite for the soul of that knight
    May as well say mass for me.

' "At the lone midnight hour, when bad spirits have power,
    In thy chamber will I be."
With that he was gone, and my lady left alone,
    And no more did I see.'

Then changed, I trow, was that bold Baron's brow,
    From the dark to the blood-red high –
'Now tell me the mien of the knight thou hast seen,
    For, by Mary, he shall die!'

'His arms shone full bright in the beacon's red light;
    His plume it was scarlet and blue;
On his shield was a hound in a silver leash bound,
    And his crest was a branch of the yew.'

'Thou liest, thou liest, thou little foot-page,
    Loud dost thou lie to me!
For that knight is cold, and low laid in the mould,
    All under the Eildon-tree.'

'Yet hear but my word, my noble lord!
  For I heard her name his name;
And that lady bright, she called the knight
  Sir Richard of Coldinghame.'

The bold Baron's brow then changed, I trow,
  From high blood-red to pale –
'The grave is deep and dark, and the corpse is stiff and stark,
  So I may not trust thy tale.

'Where fair Tweed flows round holy Melrose,
  And Eildon slopes to the plain,
Full three nights ago, by some secret foe,
  That gay gallant was slain.

'The varying light deceived thy sight,
  And the wild winds drown'd the name;
For the Dryburgh bells ring and the white monks do sing
  For Sir Richard of Coldinghame!'

He pass'd the court-gate, and he oped the tower-grate,
  And he mounted the narrow stair
To the bartizan-seat, where, with maids that on her wait
  He found his lady fair.

That lady sat in mournful mood,
  Look'd over hill and vale,

Over Tweed's fair flood and Mertoun's wood
And all down Teviotdale.

'Now hail, now hail, thou lady bright!'
'Now hail, thou Baron true!
What news what news from Ancram fight?
What news from the bold Buccleuch?'

'The Ancram Moor is red with gore,
For many a southron fell;
And Buccleuch has charged us evermore
To watch our beacons well.'

The lady blush'd red, but nothing she said;
Nor added the Baron a word
Then she stepp'd down the stair to her chamber fair,
And so did her moody lord.

In sleep the lady mourn'd, and the Baron toss'd and turn'd,
And oft to himself he said,
'The worms around him creep, and his bloody grave is
deep –
It cannot give up the dead!'

It was near the ringing of matin-bell,
The night was wellnigh done,
When a heavy sleep on that Baron fell,
34   On the eve of good Saint John.

The lady look'd through the chamber fair,
  By the light of a dying flame;
And she was aware of a knight stood there –
  Sir Richard of Coldinghame!

'Alas! away, away!' she cried,
  'For the holy Virgin's sake!'
'Lady, I know who sleeps by thy side;
  But, lady, he will not awake.

'By Eildon-tree, for long nights three,
  In bloody grave have I lain;
The mass and the death-prayer are said for me,
  But, lady, they are said in vain.

'By the Baron's brand, near Tweed's fair strand,
  Most foully slain I fell;
And my restless sprite on the beacon's height
  For a space is doom'd to dwell.

'At our trysting-place, for a certain space,
  I must wander to and fro;
But I had not had power to come to thy bower
  Had'st thou not conjured me so.'

Love master'd fear; her brow she cross'd –
  'How, Richard, hast thou sped?

And art thou saved, or art thou lost?'
  The vision shook his head!

'Who spilleth life shall forfeit life;
  So bid thy lord believe:
That lawless love is guilt above,
  This awful sign receive.'

He laid his left palm on an oaken beam,
  His right upon her hand –
The lady shrunk, and fainting sunk,
  For it scorch'd like a fiery brand.

The sable score of fingers four
  Remains on that board impress'd;
And for evermore that lady wore
  A covering on her wrist.

There is a nun in Dryburgh bower,
  Ne'er looks upon the sun;
There is a monk in Melrose tower,
  He speaketh word to none;

That nun who ne'er beholds the day,
  That monk who speaks to none –
That nun was Smaylho'me's Lady gay,
  That monk the bold Baron.

Hunting Song

Waken, lords and ladies gay,
On the mountain dawns the day,
All the jolly chase is here,
With hawk, and horse, and hunting-spear!
Hounds are in their couples yelling,
Hawks are whistling, horns are knelling,
Merrily, merrily, mingle they,
'Waken, lords and ladies gay.'

Waken, lords and ladies gay,
The mist has left the mountain grey,
Springlets in the dawn are steaming,
Diamonds on the brake are gleaming:
And foresters have busy been,
To track the buck in thicket green;
Now we come to chant our lay,
'Waken, lords and ladies gay.'

Waken, lords and ladies gay,
To the greenwood haste away;
We can show you where he lies,
Fleet of foot, and tall of size;
We can show the marks he made,
When 'gainst the oak his antlers fray'd;
You shall see him brought to bay,
'Waken, lords and ladies gay.'

Louder, louder chant the lay,
Waken, lords and ladies gay!
Tell them youth, and mirth, and glee,
Run a course as well as we;
Time, stern huntsman! who can baulk,
Stanch as hound, and fleet as hawk:
Think of this, and rise with day,
Gentle lords and ladies gay.

Lullaby of an Infant Chief

O hush thee, my babie, thy sire was a knight,
Thy mother a lady, both lovely and bright;
The woods and the glens, from the towers which we see,
They all are belonging, dear babie, to thee.
    O ho ro, i ri ri, cadul gu lo,
    O ho ro, i ri ri, &c

O fear not the bugle, though loudly it blows,
It calls but the warders that guard thy repose;
Their bows would be bended, their blades would be red,
Ere the step of a foeman drew near to thy bed.
    O ho ro, i ri ri, &c.

O hush thee, my babie, the time soon will come
When thy sleep shall be broken by trumpet and drum;
Then hush thee, my darling, take rest while you may,

For strife comes with manhood, and waking with day.
    O ho ro, i ri ri, &c.

Jock of Hazeldean

'Why weep ye by the tide, ladie?
    Why weep ye by the tide?
I'll wed ye to my youngest son,
    And ye sall be his bride:
And ye sall be his bride, ladie,
    Sae comely to be seen' –
But aye she loot the tears down fa'
    For Jock of Hazeldean.

'Now let this wilfu' grief be done,
    And dry that cheek so pale;
Young Frank is chief of Errington,
    And lord of Langley-dale;
His step is first in peaceful ha',
    His sword in battle keen' –
But aye she loot the tears down fa'
    For Jock of Hazeldean.

'A chain of gold ye sall not lack,
    Nor braid to bind your hair;
Nor mettled hound, not managed hawk,
    Nor palfrey fresh and fair;

And you, the foremost o' them a',
   Shall ride our forest queen' –
But aye she loot the tears down fa'
   For Jock of Hazeldean.

The kirk was deck'd at morning-tide,
   The tapers glimmer'd fair;
The priest and bridegroom wait the bride,
   And dame and knight are there.
They sought her baith by bower and ha';
   The ladie was not seen!
She's o'er the Border, and awa'
   Wi' Jock of Hazeldean.

Pibroch of Donuil Dhu

Pibroch of Donuil Dhu,
   Pibroch of Donuil,
Wake thy wild voice anew,
   Summon Clan-Conuil.
Come away, come away,
   Hark to the summons!
Come in your war array,
   Gentles and commons.

Come from deep glen, and
   From mountain so rocky,

The war-pipe and pennon
　Are at Inverlochy.
Come every hill-plaid, and
　True heart that wears one,
Come every steel blade, and
　Strong hand that bears one.

Leave untended the herd,
　The flock without shelter;
Leave the corpse uninterr'd,
　The bride at the altar;
Leave the deer, leave the steer,
　Leave nets and barges:
Come with your fighting gear,
　Broadswords and targes.

Come as the winds come, when
　Forests are rended,
Come as the waves come, when
　Navies are stranded:
Faster come, faster come,
　Faster and faster,
Chief, vassal, page and groom,
　Tenant and master.

Fast they come, fast they come;
　See how they gather!
Wide waves the eagle plume,

Blended with heather.
Cast your plaids, draw your blades,
   Forward, each man, set!
Pibroch of Donuil Dhu,
   Knell for the onset!

Nora's Vow

Hear what Highland Nora said, –
'The Earlie's son I will not wed,
Should all the race of nature die,
And none be left but he and I.
For all the gold, for all the gear,
And all the lands both far and near
That ever valour lost or won,
I would not wed the Earlie's son.'

'A maiden's vows,' old Callum spoke,
'Are lightly made and lightly broke;
The heather on the mountain's height
Begins to bloom in purple light;
The frost-wind soon shall sweep away
That lustre deep from glen and brae;
Yet Nora, ere its bloom be gone,
May blithely wed the Earlie's son.'

'The swan,' she said, 'the lake's clear breast
May barter for the eagle's nest;
The Awe's fierce stream may backward turn,
Ben-Cruaichan fall, and crush Kilchurn;
Our kilted clans, when blood is high,
Before their foes may turn and fly;
But I, were all these marvels done,
Would never wed the Earlie's son.'

Still in the water-lily's shade
Her wonted nest the wild-swan made;
Ben-Cruaichan stands as fast as ever,
Still downward foams the Awe's fierce river;
To shun the clash of foeman's steel
No Highland brogue has turn'd the heel;
But Nora's heart is lost and won,
– She's wedded to the Earlie's son!

from WAVERLEY

Gellatley's Song to the Deerhounds

Hie away, hie away,
Over bank and over brae,
Where the copsewood is the greenest,
Where the fountains glisten sheenest,
Where the lady-fern grows strongest,
Where the morning dew lies longest,
Where the black-cock sweetest sips it,
Where the fairy latest trips it;
Hie to haunts right seldom seen,
Lovely, lonesome, cool, and green,
Over bank and over brae,
Hie away, hie away.

from THE HEART OF MIDLOTHIAN

'*Proud Maisie is in the wood*'

Proud Maisie is in the wood,
   Walking so early;
Sweet Robin sits on the bush,
   Singing so rarely.

'Tell me, thou bonny bird,
   When shall I marry me?'
'When six braw gentlemen
   Kirkward shall carry ye.'

'Who makes the bridal bed,
   Birdie, say truly?'
'The grey-headed sexton
   That delves the grave duly.

'The glow-worm o'er grave and stone
   Shall light thee steady.
The owl from the steeple sing,
   "Welcome, proud lady." '

from THE BRIDE OF LAMMERMOOR

Lucy Ashton's Song

Lucy Ashton *sings*: –

Look not thou on beauty's charming,
Sit thou still when kings are arming,
Taste not when the wine-cup glistens,
Speak not when the people listens,
Stop thine ear against the singer,
From the red gold keep thy finger;
Vacant heart and hand and eye,
Easy live and quiet die.

from IVANHOE

The Barefooted Friar

I'll give thee, good fellow, a twelve-month or twain,
To search Europe through from Byzantium to Spain;
But ne'er shall you find, should you search till you tire,
So happy a man as the Barefooted Friar.

Your knight for his lady pricks forth in career,
And is brought home at even-song prick'd through with a
     spear;
I confess him in haste – for his lady desires
No comfort on earth save the Barefooted Friar's.

Your monarch? – Pshaw! many a prince has been known
To barter his robes for our cowl and our gown;
But which of us e'er felt the idle desire
To exchange for a crown the grey hood of a Friar?

The Friar has walk'd out, and where'er he has gone,
The land and its fatness is mark'd for his own;

He can roam where he lists, he can stop when he tires,
For every man's house is the Barefooted Friar's.

He's expected at noon, and no wight, till he comes,
May profane the great chair, or the porridge of plums;
For the best of the cheer, and the seat by the fire,
Is the undenied right of the Barefooted Friar.

He's expected at night, and the pasty's made hot,
They broach the brown ale, and they fill the black pot;
And the goodwife would wish the goodman in the mire,
Ere he lack'd a soft pillow, the Barefooted Friar.

Long flourish the sandal, the cord, and the cope,
The dread of the devil and trust of the Pope!
For to gather life's roses, unscathed by the brier,
Is granted alone to the Barefooted Friar.

from QUENTIN DURWARD

County Guy

Ah! County Guy, the hour is nigh,
    The sun has left the lea,
The orange flower perfumes the bower,
    The breeze is on the sea.
The lark, his lay who thrill'd all day,
    Sits hush'd his partner nigh;
Breeze, bird, and flower, confess the hour,
    But where is County Guy?

The village maid steals through the shade,
    Her shepherd's suit to hear;
To beauty shy, by lattice high,
    Sings high-born Cavalier.
The star of Love, all stars above,
    Now reigns o'er earth and sky;
And high and low the influence know,
    But where is County Guy!

from 'THE DOOM OF DEVORGOIL'

'Bonny Dundee'

To the Lords of Convention 'twas Claver'se who spoke,
'Ere the King's crown shall fall there are crowns to be
    broke;
So let each Cavalier who loves honour and me,
Come follow the bonnet of Bonny Dundee.

   'Come fill up my cup, come fill up my can,
   Come saddle your horses, and call up your men;
   Come open the West Port, and let me gang free,
   And it's room for the bonnets of Bonny Dundee!'

Dundee he is mounted, he rides up the street,
The bells are rung backward, the drums they are beat;
But the Provost, douce man, said, 'Just e'en let him be,
The Gude Town is weel quit of that Deil of Dundee.'

50   Come fill up my cup, &c.

As he rode down the sanctified bends of the Bow,
Ilk carline was flyting and shaking her pow;
But the young plants of grace they look'd couthie and slee,
Thinking, 'Luck to thy bonnet, thou Bonny Dundee!'

Come fill up my cup, &c.

With sour-featured Whigs the Grass-market was cramm'd
As if half the West had set tryst to be hang'd;
There was spite in each look, there was fear in each e'e,
As they watch'd for the bonnets of Bonny Dundee.

Come fill up my cup, &c.

These cowls of Kilmarnock had spits and had spears,
And lang-hafted gullies to kill Cavaliers;
But they shrunk to close-heads, and the causeway was free,
At the toss of the bonnet of Bonny Dundee.

Come fill up my cup, &c.

He spurr'd to the foot of the proud Castle rock,
And with the gay Gordon he gallantly spoke;
'Let Mons Meg and her marrows speak twa words or three,
For the love of the bonnet of Bonny Dundee.'

Come fill up my cup, &c.

The Gordon demands of him which way he goes—
'Where'er shall direct me the shade of Montrose!

Your Grace in short space shall hear tidings of me,
Or that low lies the bonnet of Bonny Dundee.

    Come fill up my cup, &c.

'There are hills beyond Pentland, and lands beyond Forth,
If there's lords in the Lowlands, there's chiefs in the North;
There are wild Duniewassals, three thousand times three,
Will cry *hoigh!* for the bonnet of Bonny Dundee.

    Come fill up my cup, &c.

'There's brass on the target of barken'd bull-hide;
There's steel in the scabbard that dangles beside;
The brass shall be burnish'd, the steel shall flash free,
At a toss of the bonnet of Bonny Dundee.

    Come fill up my cup, &c.

'Away to the hills, to the caves, to the rocks –
Ere I own an usurper, I'll couch with the fox;
And tremble, false Whigs, in the midst of your glee,
You have not seen the last of my bonnet and me!'

    Come fill up my cup, &c.

He waved his proud hand, and the trumpets were blown,
The kettle-drums clash'd, and the horsemen rode on,
Till on Ravelston's cliffs and on Clermiston's lee,
Died away the wild war-notes of Bonny Dundee.

Come fill up my cup, come fill up my can,
Come saddle the horses and call up the men,
Come open your gates, and let me gae free,
For it's up with the bonnets of Bonny Dundee!

A Note on Sir Walter Scott

Sir Walter Scott (1771–1832), Scottish novelist, historian, and poet, born in Edinburgh, where his father was a lawyer. He was educated at the High School of Edinburgh and Edinburgh University. He became a lawyer and in 1799 was appointed a sheriff-depute of Selkirkshire, while in the same year he published his first book, a metrical translation of Burger's *Lenore*, which drew considerable attention to the young writer. Three years later, when he issued the *Minstrelsy of the Scottish Border* (two volumes), consisting of old ballads he had collected in the border country, popular interest in him began to grow rapidly. Meanwhile he was busy with more original work, and in 1805 he published a long narrative poem, *The Lay of the Last Minstrel*. In 1808 he followed this with a similar work, *Marmion*, succeeded in 1809 by *The Lady of the Lake*. These metrical stories had an instant and wide success, and made their author considerably wealthy. With this money he supplied half the capital for starting the publishing house of Ballantyne, and in 1812 went to live at Abbotsford, near Melrose.

Scott's first novel was *Waverley*, issued anonymously in 1814. It was followed by *Guy Mannering*, 1815, *The Antiquary* and *Old Mortality*, 1816, *The Heart of Midlothian*, 1818, *Ivanhoe*, 1829, and *The Monastery* and *The Abbott*, 1820. They were widely read with almost as much enthusiasm in France as in England. For years the secret of the authorship was kept, since Scott considered novel-writing below the dignity of an eminent lawyer and country gentleman, but eventually it leaked out. In 1820 he was created a baronet, and in the same year was elected president of the Royal Society of Scotland, while Abbotsford began to attract visitors from far and near. In 1821 he published *Kenilworth*, and between 1821 and 1828 wrote many novels, among the most popular being *Quentin Durward*, 1823, *Redgauntlet*, 1824, *The Betrothed* and *The Talisman*, 1825, and *Woodstock*, 1826.

Misfortune then overtook him. In 1826 the firm of Ballantyne was made bankrupt, with liabilities of over a quarter of a million pounds. How far Scott was legally responsible is a matter of controversy (see E. Quayle, *The Ruin of Sir Walter Scott*, 1968), but he felt himself under a moral obligation to satisfy the firm's creditors, and at the age of 55 set himself the heroic task of paying off this enormous debt. His *Journal* is a moving record of his intimate thoughts under this burden. Writing with his accustomed speed, he produced *The Fair Maid of Perth*, 1828, and *Anne of Geierstein*, 1829. He also compiled a life of Napoleon, 1827, and in the same year published the first

series of his *Tales of a Grandfather*, a history of Scotland. The second series followed in 1828; but the author's powers were failing, and his last two novels, *Castle Dangerous*, 1832, and *Count Robert of Paris*, 1832, are much inferior. Scott's health was giving way, and he went to the Continent to recuperate. He returned home to die, and was buried at Dryburgh Abbey.

Scott exerted a strong influence on the imaginative life of his country. Before his time Scottish history was virtually unknown to the public, but among the results of the Waverley novels was the founding of numerous learned societies, in particular the Abbotsford and Bannatyne Clubs, whose members found and published documents illustrating Scotland's past. Scott also materially affected the literary movement of his time: his unconventional manner of writing and his total freedom from the academic point of view were largely instrumental in arousing the French Romantic Movement which produced such writers as Hugo, de Musset, and Gautier, and painters such as Diaz, Dupré, Corot, and Millet. Scott was also the creator of the historical novel, combining the naturalness and realism of writers like Fielding with the historical and romantic element of adventure and the marvels of superstition. His influence on Balzac was acknowledged. Critics have suggested that the historical romance had a damaging effect on the writing of history as exemplified by Carlyle's *French Revolution*. But Scott himself never confounded fiction and history, though he took the greatest liberty with

facts. His greatest novels were those with a background of 17th- and 18th-century Scotland. It has been said that his closest affinities were not with the romantic novelists of his time, but with the great 18th-century novelists and their predecessor, Cervantes.

Other titles in this series